# *NOW I SEE*

Juvens Nsabimana

ISBN: 978-1-9161880-6-8

Any references to historical events, real people, or
real places are used fictitiously. Names, characters,
and places are products of the author's imagination

First printed edition 2024

www.juvensnsabimana.com

# CAPTIVE OF THE SYSTEM

*Should I own a card as my identity?*
*Numbers define who I am*
*I am a captive of the system*

*Should I carry a book*
*when visiting a brother?*
*Numbers label me*
*as one of the land,*
*They are keys to enter elsewhere*
*I am a captive of the system*

*Should I belong to any country?*
*Borders drawn by man,*
*Land owned by authorities*
*we on the earth are only*
*captives of their system*

*Should there be governments?*
*A group of men*
*like everyone else,*
*were born,*
*once infants, toddlers, and teens,*
*now create laws.*
*I, under man's law, am just*
*a captive of the system.*

*Should I obey the law?*
*Rules controlling my actions,*

*Power wielded against me.*
*A governed man has no advantage*
*over a babysat child.*
*I'm a captive of the system.*

*Should there be a ruler?*
*One with authority over us all,*
*above all living beings*
*I need not climb the mountain*
*to reach him at the peak.*
*He must come down,*
*to understand life at the valley, or*
*I will always be a captive of his system.*

# *REVOLUTION*

*The Revolution has come to end our illusion*
*we'd been lost in confusion*
*we're products of oppression*
*Madness clouded our contemplation*
*all we need is revolution*

*The Revolution has come to end our*
*alienation*
*we, the needy,*
*facing discrimination*
*In men's judgments,*
*our children discredited,*
*theirs praised with reputation*
*No more giving them our attention*
*We need only their provocation*
*We, the angry, bring the revolution*

*The Revolution has come to our ghettos*
*to topple their mansions*
*Our rage targeting their strongholds*
*Ghostly units, breaking isolation*
*ending the corrupt administration*

*Now is the revolution*
*The fall of their organization*
*Continuation of our demonstration*
*The journey to our destination*

*We march in the uptown streets,*
*bringing change to the nation*

*It's the Revolution by the fearless stallions*
*Decriminalizing the oppressed*
*The solution to a long-standing situation*
*It's the Revolution*

# *SEEKING TRUTH*

*Bound by the chains of slavery*
*Doubts filled my mind*
*Fear seized my heart*
*The world was dark*
*Nights covered days,*
*If truth sets a man free*
*I'd do nothing else*
*but seek it.*

*Sitting in the front row at church,*
*expecting freedom in my thoughts,*
*love in my heart*
*life in my soul*
*I found another truth,*
*No way, no truth, no life*
*ever found there*
*I'd do nothing else*
*but keep seeking truth.*

*Leapt from church to the streets,*
*wanting to fit in and*
*hear what others say*
*Heard from a mix of*
*wise and unwise,*
*skilled and unskilled,*
*only illusions living in their minds*
*I'd do nothing else*
*but keep seeking truth.*

*On the street,*
*I bought the latest newspapers,*
*reading a politician's words*
*but the controlled press*
*almost led me to despair with*
*its rope of lies,*
*trying to choke me*
*like millions before me*
*I did nothing*
*but keep seeking truth.*

*A few steps from the street,*
*I entered a pub,*
*intending to drown my troubles*
*Thought I'd find truth*
*but shared drinks with men*
*drowning in their own troubles*
*I'd do nothing else*
*but keep seeking truth*

*When the sun set,*
*I returned home, very tired*
*still searching for truth*
*Turned on the television for news,*
*saw no truth in it*
*only bitter lies and hypocrisy,*
*hatred and violence*
*from slave-drivers and power-seekers*
*I'd do nothing else*
*but keep seeking truth.*

*Opened a book,*
*saw a glimpse of truth*
*but was not freed*
*Closed my eyes*
*Sailed my mind to my heart*
*There I found truth and*
*I'm free now.*

*I had been blind to those men*
*reaching me anytime they wanted,*
*Now I can see*
*I had been a puppet*
*doing what they wanted*
*Now I've withdrawn*
*I had been mute,*
*no words from my mouth*
*Now I can speak*
*I had been in chains of lies*
*Now I am free*
*Truth has been found.*

# THAT CHILD

*If there had never been*
*political indoctrination*
*in that child's head,*
*he wouldn't grow up*
*believing in a party,*
*disbelieving in unity*
*Trusting a flag,*
*distrusting nature,*
*Embracing politics,*
*disgracing community*
*How many fathers and mothers*
*would he have now?*
*How many brothers and sisters*
*would he have now?*
*But he's all alone*

*If there had never been*
*religious belief*
*in that child's heart,*
*he wouldn't grow up*
*trusting one book,*
*distrusting neighbors*
*Sinking in popery,*
*drowning in shahada*
*How many fathers and mothers*
*would he have now?*
*How many brothers and sisters*

*would he have now?*
*But he's all alone*

*If there had never been*
*cultural conditioning*
*in that child's head,*
*he wouldn't have adopted*
*societal norms and taboos*
*No tribes, no ethnicity*
*He would be a bard,*
*now he's barbaric*
*How many fathers and mothers*
*would he have now?*
*How many brothers and sisters*
*would he have now?*
*But he's all alone*

*If there had never been*
*formal education*
*that fooled my child's mind,*
*erased all his wisdom,*
*planted ego in its place*
*Education that*
*locked him in a small room*
*while he could have the whole universe*
*He could have performed*
*Thousands of miracles on earth,*
*now he has nothing at all*
*All his talents wasted*
*All his gifts stolen.*

## CAN'T FIT IN

*I walked into the pub*
*People indulged in wines and whiskeys*
*Eyes on the sports screen,*
*eyes on women's figures*
*What noise in my ears!*
*They came to buy happiness*
*but I'm happy without cost*
*I can't fit in*

*Entered the grand hall*
*built for men of Christ,*
*that's the church*
*They sit*
*listen to speeches*
*Don't understand?*
*No questions allowed*
*I see lions*
*transformed into sheep*
*in the fold*
*Little sheep,*
*pay and leave*
*The shepherd said*
*I can't fit in*
*I'd rather be a dead lion*

*As a boy,*
*I visited my friend's home*
*Friends gathered,*
*sat on couches,*

*each with a device*
*They do nothing*
*but watch, like, follow,*
*comment, and subscribe*
*I want to talk,*
*all seem deaf*
*Entertainers, adultery*
*Politicians, and idiotic games*
*captivate them*
*I can't fit in*

*Got a good job,*
*Job security*
*No one with a desk job wants more*
*Satisfied with earnings*
*Can take a loan*
*Can buy a house*
*Can start a family*
*Can work for life*
*my mind limited to salary*
*No, I can't fit in*
*I'm leaving*

# I AM A FOOL

*How foolish I am
to idolize the dominant creatures on the
peak,
the ones who brought darkness to earth
How they laugh
while children cry
Feeding their fellow wealthy
while the poor go hungry
Why do I sit down
and give them my precious hour
when they ruin lives?
I am a fool, I am a fool
but I am not alone.*

*How foolish I am
to worship the dominant creatures on the
peak
how I praise them
when all they do is destroy me,
when oil barrels are valued more
than my life
How can I speak of them?
How dare they
decide my fate?
How I was discarded like trash
I am a fool, I am a fool
but I am not alone.*

*How foolish I am*
*to respect the dominant creatures on the peak,*
*the ones who slaughtered living beings.*
*How foolish I am,*
*hanging their portraits above me*
*How foolish I am*
*to freeze my body for their passage.*
*How foolish we are*
*to make them*
*our constant topic of conversation*
*How foolish I am*
*to allow my child to study them*
*I am a fool, I am a fool*
*but I am not alone.*

*How foolish I am*
*to worship the dominant creatures on the peak.*
*How foolish I am*
*to let them reduce me to a submissive boy*
*How foolish I am*
*to relinquish control of my life.*
*How foolish I am*
*to let them shape me into*
*a product of their dark deeds*
*I am a fool, I am a fool*
*but I am not alone.*

*How foolish I am*
*to idolize the dominant creatures on the*

*peak.*
*How foolish I am*
*to allow them to turn me into a follower*
*If I am to be their faithful follower,*
*I'd be the fire following the gas*
*until both of us pollute the air*

## ALL HUMANS

*All humans are created equal,*
*I don't think so*
*I was not born nor created equal to you*
*You took your first breath in the hospital,*
*lay in a crib*
*I came into the world in the wild*
*You can be certified*
*I can be untamed*

*All humans are created equal,*
*I don't think so*
*You were created with plenty,*
*the city welcomed you warmly*
*I was created with scarcity,*
*the city abandoned me*
*Some of you were created with fame*
*Some of us in obscurity*
*like lost vagrants in a dark forest*

*All humans are created equal,*
*I don't think so*
*You were created privileged,*
*with superiority*
*I was created with disadvantages*
*Some of you were created into prig money*
*regime*
*Some of us from worthless peasants*

*All humans are created equal,*
*I don't think so*
*Some of you were created in Beverly Hills*
*At eighteen,*
*You found yourselves at Harvard College*
*Some of us created in Makoko Slums*
*At eighteen,*
*We found ourselves cold in the culvert*

*All humans are created equal,*
*I don't think so*
*You were created insured,*
*life was guaranteed*
*I was created jobless,*
*death was guaranteed*

# *HYPOCRITES*

*All our trust was thrown at*
*the hypocrites*
*All our hopes came from*
*the dishonesties*
*All our beliefs fell on us from*
*the ignoramuses*
*Now, our lives rest in the hands of*
*the rulers*
*who repaid our love with hate*

*Shame on our ancestors*
*The nincompoops honored invaders*
*Lives were lost*
*through the door of no return*
*Now, the remainders of lives lie*
*in the hands of predators*

*Christianity,*
*The tool of those leeches*
*who drained knowledge*
*from our sincere minds*
*Now, we are all beggars*
*Our children are fading,*
*Blood sucked by leeches*

*Hypocrites turned brothers into strangers*
*Hypocrites turned friends into foes*
*Hypocrites made us all helpless fools*

*Hypocrites introduced hunger to us*
*Looking up but our eyes see nothing*
*but hypocritical power over us*

# THE TRUTH

*The truth reveals,*
*Violence is now successful*
*It has always been successful*
*Success is desired by all,*
*I choose loss*
*if I am to be violent for success*

*The truth is,*
*God remains at their heart's core,*
*Only if he can be oppressed*
*Can he feel the pain I feel?*
*Only if he's more suffering than I,*
*He's the seed within my soul.*

*Truth speaks,*
*Politics and Religion claim eternal victory,*
*They captured me*
*through money and media,*
*I've always been their servant*
*like my father before me,*
*Only if politics stand for humanity,*
*Only if religion stands for peace and love,*
*I'll worship wealth*

*Truth uncovers,*
*Anything that opposed governance*
*and faith had been hell of boob*

*Only if they welcome universal human
nature,
Only if they heed my truth,
I'll stub out my cigarette,
empty my bottle of whiskey and
honor the legislator and reverend.*

## YOU OWNED ME

*At birth*
*No choice was mine*
*You documented me in papers*
*Birth certificate*
*You owned me*

*At five,*
*I consented*
*To Sunday school I went*
*You began to confuse*
*You owned me*

*At seven,*
*I agreed*
*to walk to school*
*You started brainwashing,*
*stealing my world,*
*pouring yours into mine,*
*You owned me*

*At twelve,*
*I agreed,*
*Learning your history,*
*You stopped me*
*from creating my own,*
*You owned me*

*At eighteen,*
*I accepted*
*To college I went,*
*Learning to be your tool*
*You owned me*

*At twenty-two,*
*I agreed,*
*Graduating proudly*
*Degree in hand,*
*Believing I was smarter*
*My essence burnt,*
*You owned me*

*At twenty-three,*
*I agreed,*
*Job secured*
*You kept making me*
*Not me making me*
*You put me under paper's power*
*Slave to money*
*Why always papers?*
*Papers everywhere*
*You owned me*

*At twenty-five,*
*I agreed*
*Dragged to another illusion*
*Marriage and legal papers*
*There wasn't any love here*
*when I love my woman*

*under laws of a man*
*Marriage certificate*
*What the hell is that for?*

*At twenty-six,*
*Another little innocent slave*
*crying just like me,*
*Coming into the world*
*you were mastering*
*You owned us*

*At twenty-seven,*
*A woman dissatisfied,*
*Distressed by your monetary system*
*Burden on my shoulder*
*I almost jumped off the bridge*
*You saved me,*
*loaning papers of yours*
*More papers, more debts*
*A better slave to your system*
*to pay you back the papers*
*you even printed*
*You owned my family*

*At thirty,*
*I agreed*
*Slaving to survive,*
*No new thoughts wanted,*
*Mind chained to salary*
*All yours,*
*You truly owned me*

*At thirty-three,*
*Darkness turns to daylight*
*Seeking my true self*
*No more acceptances*
*My child won't lose like me*
*I'm a man*
*I'm the world of man*
*against your heartless world,*
*No longer owned by you*

*Emancipation now*
*from your lifelong slavery*
*You, slaving men*
*from birth to death*
*I'm standing firm, criticizing,*
*You no more thinking for me*
*Disillusioned,*
*Came to reason like a man,*
*Though standing against you*
*seems to stand against the whole world*
*I stand still beyond*
*the level of the history you created*

## WOMAN, MAN

*A woman brings life*
*A man brings death*
*If birth should cease,*
*so should killing*

*A woman wants heaven*
*A man wants hell.*
*With man in power*
*The world is nothing but hell*

*A woman talks*
*A man is silent*
*Silence is strength,*
*Strength is man's*
*Weakness is woman's*

*A woman shapes a child's early years*
*A man shapes the child's situation*
*A child becomes a battlefield*
*between mother and father*

*In trouble,*
*A woman fears*
*A man rages.*
*Anger acts*
*Fear freezes*

*If a woman weakens a man,*
*Later, he strengthens her,*
*Both are weak.*

*A woman thinks with her heart*
*A man with his mind*
*Her thoughts are clearer*

*A woman loves words*
*A man loves sight*
*He speaks to please*
*She shines to attract*
*The weakest man is talkative,*
*The strongest woman is a magnet for men's*
*eyes*

## *ART*

*Art is everything*
*The mightiest weapon*
*to defeat the powerful,*
*to challenge oppressors*

*From heart to brain,*
*Art creates a bright world*
*in this dark world*
*Without art, no paradise*

*Art defies law,*
*Limitless and free*
*Censoring art means less freedom*

*Art is the world,*
*the artist its creator*
*Let children sing and dance*
*Paint and draw*
*Write and rhyme*
*Once a child is made of an art*
*Peace surrounds us*
*as air cover the earth*

*With art, no war,*
*In our hands, prosperity*
*With art, no wishes,*
*No wishes, no ego*
*No ego, no hatred,*

*Only happiness and love*
*Art streams goodness,*
*Opposes evil*

*With art,*
*No need for schooling*
*that steals our knowledge*
*No need for churches*
*those turn us into sheep*
*No need to follow man's laws*
*that makes us bow*

*With art,*
*Freedom is everywhere*
*An artist is free,*
*The world is free*

## 21st CENTURY

21st Century,
Leave us now, leave,
Look at your impact:
Power shifted to women,
Men weakened
worshipping false idols,
Children seeing mannequins
not role models,
Figures and faces
diminishing male strength

21st Century,
Hurry, leave
You brought filthy music
Men lost creativity
Hearts untouched
Souls unhealed
Minds unfed
Poetry forgotten
Puppets leading the stage
I'm frozen here like
I'm mired in mud,
awaiting songs of rebellion
to challenge tyrants and feel happy

21st Century,
Go, just go
You turned men into skivvies,
Slaving for money,

*I'm longing for 10<sup>th</sup> century*
*when a man was worth*
*even if he wasn't wealthy,*
*even if he had no political power*

*21st Century, leave us be*
*Let us be human,*
*I need my natural state*
*Machines and devices mislead*
*Lost, we face biting dogs*
*21st Century, Leave now*

# *JUDGE*

*Your honor,*
*I give you no honor*
*I know you're scorner*
*Empowered to imprison me*
*Gavel in one hand*
*Lives in the other hand*
*Some end in death*
*Sentences endless*
*Injustice reigns and*
*You float on your bed.*
*They call you "your honor,"*
*We rise when you enter*
*Sit when you sit*
*Silence when commanded*
*All eyes up at you,*
*A king on his throne,*
*looking down as if that God on earth*
*In long robes,*
*Serving laws*
*forged to conquer us,*
*Educated men speak,*
*The jury decides*
*who is wrong, who is right*
*No lawyer frankly wrong or right,*
*Just less or more clever*
*Case closed*
*Suffering continues*
*Without law,*
*No outlaws*

*No crimes,*
*No defendants*
*No accusers*
*No witnesses*
*No prisons*
*No judgment*
*Only truth*
*Judge,*
*Without your job,*
*We find peace*
*When you're unemployed*
*Justice prevails*
*Don't judge me,*
*Judge yourself*

## THE SPEECH

*Let them talk,*
*Let them go on and on*
*Let cameras capture them*
*Let them appear everywhere*
*Let their voices reach every ear*
*Let them decide each life's course*
*Let the unwise applaud for them*
*They will never reach me*

*Don't want to learn from history?*
*Listen to a politician*
*Don't want to embrace the present?*
*Hear his speech clearly*
*Don't want to face a brighter future?*
*Never miss his words*

*Unrealistic men always have*
*something to say,*
*and the deaf, dumb,*
*and blind elect them*
*You, fans of speeches,*
*believing in myths*
*No longer thinking for yourselves*
*but letting speeches think for you*

*They speak,*
*Nothing is done*
*More is promised*
*Shiny promises for their children*
*They speak,*
*Good people are hated*
*Bad ones loved*
*They speak,*
*You start hating your brother*
*while they care for neither of you*
*They speak,*
*You embrace wrong, shun right*
*They speak,*
*You become inhuman*

## WHERE I BELONG

*I crossed the border*
*Searching for brothers in another land*
*but their eyes on me like herons*
*watching a snake*
*I was no warlock,*
*no colonizer,*
*no thief*
*They whispered in their tongue,*
*Knowing I couldn't understand*

*In the slums,*
*They gossiped*
*about the new bastard*
*On hills of affluence,*
*they saw danger*
*in an informal-looking man on foot*
*as if walking meant poverty,*
*Driving meant wealth*

*In a coffee shop,*
*I sat for a cup*
*beside a colored man*
*who thought he was white*
*He moved away,*
*Yet we both knew*
*We were both colored*

*No one as white as milk*
*No blood is white.*

*I spoke my mind,*
*they ran away*
*They thought me ignorant cause*
*I spoke truths that could kill me,*
*risking my own people*
*Later, they saw*
*my truth didn't kill their vibe,*
*Made me a hero*
*When death comes,*
*They'll be busy*
*until my funeral,*
*dressed in shining black*

*Where do I belong? Who to trust?*
*I belong here,*
*with my pen and pad*
*I belong here,*
*Deep in my heart*
*Trust no one but myself*

# *IN OUR OLD NEIGHBORHOOD AGAIN*

*In our old neighborhood again,*
*No more old man patting my shoulder,*
*No strength given*
*No more laughter on children's faces*
*No more women's joy in the day*

*Going to fish,*
*no more fish to catch tonight*
*as none were caught last night*
*We do what we used to,*
*Sitting in rusty iron houses*
*in our forgotten corner*
*where life is hard,*
*survival harder*

*Raising my eyes,*
*I see men*
*watching leaves fall on hills,*
*Sipping fine wine,*
*Shaking hands on our heads,*
*Sucking blood from our veins*
*Tomorrow,*
*They'll do it again*

*If peace starts at death,*
*war starts at birth.*
*We've been forgotten*
*Dead for decades*
*Eaten alive by beasts*
*Some of us stay, exhausted*

*We can be lions*
*No more heads bowed*
*No more accepting death*
*They lack what we now have:*
*Unity and numbers*
*No more dying alive,*
*We are alive, we have life*

## ME ALONE

*The world's too noisy in my ears*
*Venomous tongues want*
*to lick at my brain*
*Minds around me fed on*
*jealousy and hate,*
*wickedness and war*
*I see death approaching,*
*I pull away, he pushes closer.*
*Nobody wants me here*
*Everything disappeared*
*Only pain and suffering remain*

*An endless battle within*
*Barely breathing*
*Strength almost gone*
*The mountain is high,*
*I need a hand to pull me up*
*Below, in the valleys,*
*hungry crocodiles wait*
*I must climb,*
*To sit atop that peak,*
*but I am helpless,*
*Only me, me alone*

*It worsens,*
*Floodgates opened*

*Rain won't stop*
*I slide on wet rocks*
*No Noah to build an ark*
*I am alone, alone now*
*No aid, no protection,*
*No ship, no life jacket,*
*Just me, me alone*

# I KILLED

*My heart escapes its spot,*
*beating hard,*
*breaking through my chest*
*Blood races in my veins*
*like adrenaline,*
*I feel nothing on my skin,*
*Only pain in my head*
*I killed a man*
*He is dead,*
*Gone from earth*
*His mother won't see him,*
*His daughter won't call "Daddy"*
*The knife was heavy,*
*Blood on my shoes,*
*He didn't deserve death*
*I was in hell,*
*Dark as the devil,*
*A killer deserving to be hanged*
*Stoned by men and women*
*My nights are sleepless,*
*cold and shaking*
*Peace blown away like smoke*
*He died once,*
*I die daily*
*I shouldn't have left home,*
*Shouldn't have left my world*

*of peace and solitude*
*I shouldn't have been bribed*
*by soulless men*
*I shouldn't have let*
*my inner friend leave,*
*Leaving me in impatience and anger*
*to kill a man*
*I shouldn't have fed my bad devils*
*in front of him*
*Now they've abandoned me*
*They've left me*

# *AS I SEE THROUGH THE WALL*

*I step out,*
*Balcony-residing*
*Feel warm breeze*
*Handsome bright morning sun*
*Luckiest to be happy today*
*Looking around,*
*Beauty everywhere*
*Homes painted white*
*Green backyards*
*under trees' shade*
*They think I'm doomed*
*cause I'm alone*

*As I see through the wall,*
*Tears of a woman*
*Sour face of a man*
*Little ones, smiles turned sorrow*
*Hero against heroine*
*Neighbors not at peace*

*Next door,*
*As I see through the wall*
*Pain of a Juliet,*
*Romeo has gone*
*All alone now*
*Daughter enters,*

*Happy with a doll,*
*Mom's smile a facade,*
*"Daddy's gone to heaven,"*
*She's lying*

*I sit,*
*Looking ahead,*
*At their neighbor's home*
*I see through the wall,*
*Rings on fingers*
*Regrets on faces*
*Happiness, a wedding memory*
*Where are the smiles?*

*My eyes closed,*
*looking within*
*Yes, I'm alone,*
*Yet happy, I am happy*

## YOU'RE DEAD

*It's easy to breathe*
*when you can,*
*Hard when you can't*
*You realize it*
*when death knocks,*
*Let the nature does its job*
*Good feelings flow*
*Heart smiles*
*Life finds another life*
*Or lose it all*
*You die each day,*
*when happiness fleeting*
*like ice melting in water,*
*When darkening your soul,*
*You're dying alive*
*until buried*
*Not truly living,*
*until you're happy,*
*Anger trips you,*
*closer to hell*
*Wickedness speeds you,*
*an inch to hell*
*Now death's arms*
*open wide,*
*You fall in his chest*
*when embracing unhappiness,*

*You're dead*
*Dead as a man in a grave*

# *FEAR*

*Eyes are set on the past,*
*Darkness hides the view*
*Turn to the future,*
*vision blurred,*
*I am afraid*
*I have fear*

*I'm in the race*
*but losing ground*
*Strength lost*
*Gasping for air,*
*barely breathing*
*Today outruns yesterday,*
*I can't win this race*
*I am afraid*
*I have fear*

*All my faith in money*
*Heart surrendered to myths*
*Knowledge to doubts*
*Words speak of sickness*
*Riches slipping away*
*like the setting sun in the west*
*Poverty approaching*
*like the morning sun in the east*
*I am afraid, I have fear*

*I was drowned,*
*Yet alive*
*I was broken,*
*Here I stand*
*Still breathing*
*I am alive.*
*Faced fear now I'm strong*
*No longer fear, but boldness*
*Running against the storm,*
*Only way through,*
*Fear's dead*

## *LET ME CRY*

*Let me cry*
*when no one see my struggle,*
*Feels good, Tears shed,*
*Heart weakens,*
*weaker*
*Mind strengthens,*
*stronger*
*Let every tear carries pain*
*I'll never cry again,*

*Let me cry*
*for the loved gone ones,*
*Let my heart breaks,*
*Grief reigns*
*No chance to see them again*
*Tears shed, feels good*
*Each tears for the lost,*
*I'll never cry again,*

*Let me cry in insignificance,*
*Forgotten, forsaken,*
*Abandoned,*
*Them greedy*
*For the money sake*
*They've thrown me out*
*I'm bigger in exclusion,*

*Each tear for rejection*
*I'll never cry again*

*Let me cry unheard,*
*I shouted,*
*My voices fell on deaf ears*
*Let me scratch my face,*
*Tear my hair,*
*Fists pound walls till they bleed*
*Let me cry*
*until soil is wet,*
*I'll never cry again*

## DARK SOUL

*I go to play,*
*I'm not happy*
*I go to work,*
*Feeling weak*
*I try to write,*
*Ideas escape me*
*I avoid idiots,*
*They're all around*
*I want to be strong,*
*I need a woman*
*Found one, lost myself,*
*Cast away like stone*
*Can I be strong?*
*Yes, but dark soul resists*
*Alone, tears shed*
*Light skin seen by all,*
*They're blind to see*
*the darkest soul*
*Inside my heart,*
*Beating with the past,*
*Haunted by nightmares*
*I don't need anyone,*
*Insecurity starts*
*when they're around*
*Loneliness attacking me,*
*Yet I'm not alone*

*Here, I sit with my demons,*
*Having a good conversation*
*They better than hypocritical friends*
*who do all they can*
*to darken my heart*
*Oh God,*
*You're the one they believe in*
*Don't let my hand grabs a gun*
*If you truly love your people*

# NO CHOICE

*No choice left but no choice*
*The path to greatness lies in difference*
*Thousands of losses lead to success*
*Failing to lose is the loss of success*
*Loss, the firstborn of risk,*
*Risk, the grandfather of success,*
*The only choice we have:*
*Risk all, lose all.*

*No choice left but no choice,*
*Believe in yourself or be devoured*
*like a zebra in a pride of lions,*
*Trust no one—government,*
*Religion, friendship*
*The only way:*
*Trust yourself, to madness,*
*risking all, losing all*

*No choice left but no choice,*
*Beaten down, rise again*
*Accept no more kicks, fists,*
*Sticks, swords, or bullets*
*No more torture*

# A WOMAN

*Like a red sun swallowed by mountains,*
*the mind lost before her nakedness*
*Like a rat over rotten peanuts,*
*thoughts disappear at her smile*
*The strongest ever made,*
*breaking rocks into stones.*

*Her slow, low voice*
*like a summer wind by the ocean,*
*Her tears freeze the burning sun*
*Her touch ignites blood like fire*
*The strongest ever made*
*A dangerous baby born*

*She helps a man to forget,*
*Travels the mind like a guide*
*while a man is a tourist within his mind*
*In a day, she cuts down a tree*
*watered for ten years,*
*You just watch it fall,*
*The strongest ever made,*

*You never wanted marriage,*
*but she did*
*Like a helpless rooster losing its head*
*before being fried*

*In bed with her,*
*Your power burned*
*The strongest ever made*

# I AM NOT THEM

*Most seek escape from danger,*
*They don't know they need more*
*to enjoy peace when it comes*
*Beaten down, I rise,*
*Facing danger head-on*

*Most are haunted by their past*
*Complaining of problems*
*Fearing the future*
*they haven't seen yet*
*Few realize all we have is today*
*I live in the present.*

*Most die for the top,*
*Yet those who step back,*
*launch like rockets,*
*Not seen until they break through*
*I choose to remain low,*
*invisible until I reach the clouds*

*Most avoid criticism,*
*They want praise for doing nothing*
*I want not worship, lots of critics*
*For I worship no human.*
*I am not them.*

## RELIGION MUST BE WORSE

*I've seen a man*
*who always prays,*
*Always unhappy*
*He prayed all his life,*
*unanswered till his last breath*
*Dosed on religious drugs,*
*His brain strayed from focus,*
*Religion must be worse than cocaine*

*I've seen a man*
*beg to an unseen force,*
*Fasting forty days, beseeching*
*like a street beggar*
*I've seen a homeless,*
*hungry child*
*Mind opened by an empty stomach,*
*Achieved what church prayers couldn't*
*Religion must be worse than problems*

*I know a man,*
*wise and spirited,*
*until he walked into a church*
*His wisdom unloaded,*
*Religion leaves no room for new ideas*

*I've seen free souls in dogs,*
*Loving heart in toddlers,*
*And darkness in those who pray devoutly*
*Believing in nothing but one book,*
*Declaring we all destined for hell*
*Hell must be better,*
*For religion keeps us from it*
*Religion must be worse than hell*

# HELL IN THE CITY

*The city,*
*A dangerous place to flee from*
*Peace hidden beyond its borders*
*Bright and colorful,*
*Its people seldom sleep*
*Never dark at night,*
*Yet, the city accommodates dark hearts*

*Living in the city,*
*See them burghers going insane*
*Goddamn, like vipers in a den,*
*Villains hunting souls to destroy*
*It's like sitting in a tunnel,*
*yearning for light you can't reach*

*A man in the city*
*Possessions in the mind*
*He's steamed up*
*when a neighbor got a lot more*
*Money got to be god*
*Bishop worship god*
*His followers must worship god*
*Even the crowned worship god*
*There's no such god for me anymore*

*A man of knowledge,*
*A creative soul,*
*A man of talent*
*should avoid the city men' eyes*
*Even cats see the fire in them*

*I love silent friends,*
*Free spirits around me*
*I am in haven as my dog*
*and kitten walk in the nature,*
*Together, we feeling*
*the green world's beauty*

*How magnificent it is*
*A week without humans*
*How great it is,*
*no more news,*
*Like walking on water,*
*never drowning*
*How powerful it is,*
*free from rulers and governors*
*How happy it is,*
*no more fake smiles,*
*no devils behind angelic faces*
*Then, I might return to the city*

# THE TROUBLED MAN

*The troubled man,*
*always needing company*
*Clever but lacking true knowledge*
*Fitting into every basket*
*Oh, troubled man,*
*You want to impress*
*those who don't care,*
*You've forgotten yourself*

*By fools eyes,*
*you're seen as*
*a whale in the ocean*
*By your own eyes,*
*You see yourself*
*as an unbreakable rock,*
*but you're just a balloon,*
*blown towards thorns*
*Believing peace found in a full wallet,*
*Hundreds of friends*
*Troubled man,*
*you run away from peace*
*trusting humans*
*You're forever troubled*

*You're in trouble without learning*
*You're in trouble*

*suppressing truth with power,*
*Forgetting a tree grows tall over years,*
*Cut down in minutes*
*You're in trouble,*
*no clue about creativity*
*You're in trouble,*
*need public education*
*You're in trouble,*
*disconnected from art*

*The most troubled,*
*You don't know you're doomed*
*Eyes set on newspapers,*
*caring for the powerful*
*who don't know you,*
*Shrinking like used soap,*
*A small fish for bigger ones*
*Herbivore for carnivores*
*Oh, troubled man, you need one thing*
*Just one thing*
*To spend time alone*

# IT WAS THE BEGINNING

*When he had no friends,*
*he had no money,*
*Thinking he lacked luck until he saw,*
*It was the beginning,*
*to earn all the money he wanted,*
*and stop making friends*

*When hope for the future lost,*
*he focused on past losses,*
*believing he was unlucky until he saw,*
*It was the beginning to get back lost hope*
*and let go of the past*

*When no space was left for him,*
*he stood outside in the cold,*
*Thinking he'd freeze and cry for help*
*until he saw,*
*It was the beginning to break doors*
*or die trying*

*When no one loved him,*
*he felt worthless and ugly*
*among the loved until he saw,*
*He didn't need love from others*
*until he loved himself,*
*Then lovers appeared*

*When happiness fled,*
*he lived in sadness,*
*he was just a morose*
*Seeing only ugly faces until he saw,*
*It was the beginning to choose happiness,*
*which came like a butterfly*
*and sadness died like a sprayed fly*

# THE LOVED, FORGOTTEN ONES

*Mornings kissed nights*
*countless times,*
*Months passed,*
*Years handed over years,*
*He hasn't called the loved ones*
*Not visited*
*Not sent a letter*
*They were his strength*
*when he was blown*
*from side to side*
*like a flag in the wind*
*He forgot the moments*
*when he was weak like*
*a feather falling*
*from a tree in summer,*
*Easily trampled*
*Only the forgotten ones saved him*
*Now he's like a ship without a captain,*
*Sinking slowly*
*All he can do now is regret*
*His heart covered in thorns*
*He's now in pain*
*They laughed with him,*
*cried with him,*
*now he cries alone*
*How foolish to love those*

*who never loved him*
*while turning his back on his blood—*
*his child, his brothers,*
*his sisters, his parents*
*He misses the loved ones*

# MY LITTLE FRIEND

*My little friend,*
*I miss you deeply*
*You were always there*
*when no one else was*
*Smiles come when I remember*
*how you jumped on my table,*
*stepping on my laptop,*
*unbothered by my work,*
*Only wanting to play*
*My sharp, energetic kitten,*
*Never tired of walking,*
*making my eyes heavy*
*while following you*
*My hand was a magnet to your soft fur,*
*Your little face's clear in my mind,*
*My heart aches,*
*remembering you're gone.*
*In my loneliness,*
*you were my only friend,*
*keeping smiles on my face*
*I can't forget your nails on my towel,*
*how you scratched furniture,*
*how you loved sleeping before me*
*Though small,*
*You snored like*
*You'd drunken too much*

*but I loved it*
*Your free soul sensed*
*the insecurities of neighbors*
*who hated you*
*as if you caused their problems*
*You were a pretty kitten,*
*Forever remembered,*
*I miss you*

# *FORWARD IS FORWARD*

*I woke this morning,*
*The sky might be beautiful as a flower,*
*But its light painful in my eyes*
*Not wanting another punishing day,*
*Another day of loss*
*Another day trials*
*Another day of tribulation*
*No strength to think of past joys*
*Can't see the good in today*
*No energy for future hope*
*I'm like a house cat lost*
*in a forest of wild hyenas*
*I wish the sun would set again,*
*to go to bed,*
*avoiding this cruel world*
*A world without mercy*
*I seem to be afraid but,*
*none of them with clue of*
*what this fear holds*
*My mind keeps questioning*
*I am speechless*
*See the world*
*The journey is painful*
*The road endless,*
*It looks like*
*no rides in this desert street*

*Legs tired*
*The journey exhaustive*
*but addictive*
*I don't need a ride,*
*I must keep walking*
*Forward is forward*

## HE'D RATHER FACE DEATH.

He saw death coming close,
Mr. Death needed his hug
Regret in him as he retreats,
Counting days and
nights of suffering,
alone in a desolate world,
eating grief
sipping from a cup of pain,
Another brother has gone
They always go
More ammunition manufactured
More sisters were gone
More M16s were made
More children were injured
More AKs were sold
More mothers were buried
He'd rather face death.

He wants to go, to leave
this world of false beauty
He can't endure more pain,
He can't bear this agony,
Suicide isn't a crime,
He thought he could do it
A man will make him die anyway
but this bitter pain delays him,

*He'd rather face death.*

*When he needed someone by his side,*
*Only death sat with him.*
*They conversed,*
*Through the shadow of death,*
*he glimpsed light*
*Fear conquered until*
*he shook a hand with Mr. Death,*
*He wasn't afraid anymore,*
*Defeated all fears*
*He doesn't just exist, he lives*
*Now he's at peace.*

## *ME AND MY BRAIN*

*Within my skull's walls,*
*is my brain*
*My only friend*
*One who understands me*
*Together, we'd go a lot crazier*
*to face this cruel world*
*When he runs out of me,*
*he sees only the awful sight*
*I sing awful songs*
*until the other friend of mine*
*that beats from my chest*
*saves us*

*My brain,*
*The liquid within me,*
*my strongest part*
*I rely on you for life,*
*you rely on me for life*
*My brain,*
*Only you can set me free,*
*Only I can set you free,*
*Only heart can set us free*

*When I'm brainless*
*It's brainstorm,*
*paralyzed by media,*

*fed by politics*
*brainwashed by schooling too long,*
*chained by religion long enough,*
*In the name of God,*
*made by their doctrine*

*Now I feel a brainwave*
*Now we're with our mindset*
*Time to break free*
*Brain, it's us*
*Let's make a move*
*No savior, helper, or aid,*
*No one knowing how long,*
*Surrounded by devils,*
*Blinded to light*
*Numberless swords and*
*spears pushed in us*
*We're still alive*

*Liquid part of me, unbreakable,*
*My strongest ally,*
*I stand with you,*
*We escape this prison now*
*The world holds no power over us,*
*It just me and you*

# DON'T STOP THE RAIN

*Nights so cold,*
*I'm not trembling,*
*Mornings colder,*
*I feel fine*
*Rain stormy*
*Some stay indoors,*
*Others count each drop*
*under shades*
*I walk peacefully*
*I want rain on me*
*Don't stop the rain*

*They hate rain,*
*I love it,*
*It washes away tears ignored*
*I smell its freshness,*
*Let it rain on me,*
*don't stop the rain*

*Storms blow*
*Thunders roar*
*Lightning strikes*
*Dark sky falls*
*Trees crash on houses*
*No living thing faces this rain,*
*All I want is more rain on me,*

*Don't stop the rain*

*I can feel it*
*I'm strong against floods*
*No need for umbrellas*
*I always wanted one,*
*never received one*
*No shade needed,*
*once desired*
*No need for rainbows,*
*just more heavy rain*
*I love walking on floods*
*Don't stop the rain*

# I STILL REMEMBER

*I still remember the day*
*before I got back my mind*
*while they thought*
*I was losing my mind*
*I couldn't walk this world,*
*I don't belong to them anymore*
*Talking to myself*
*when ears fell deaf,*
*Watching myself*
*when eyes were blind*
*Now eyes are on me,*
*Just cause I got back my mind*
*Crazed by their acts*
*They think I'm insane*
*I came to my senses*
*It's just me*
*not thinking like them*

*I still remember when*
*I forgot everything*
*they instilled in me*
*Everything's gone*
*my world stays,*
*They think I'm insane*
*I came to my senses*
*Craziness my nature,*

*Disgust to them unnatural*

*I still remember when*
*I disappeared*
*from their so-called light,*
*darkening my days,*
*No return,*
*Became a psychic in their eyes*
*Now don't want to be normal,*
*Wanting distance*
*from their world,*
*To stay in mine,*
*It's who I am*

# MY TEARS

*Slowly, my tears fall*
*like raindrops on pane of glass,*
*Pooling in sand at my feet,*
*creating mud,*
*I cover it with dry sand*
*I had deep pain, unhealed*
*Lost from room of happiness,*
*Now the last tear sheds,*
*No more crying.*

*Ears never heard*
*I love you*
*Body never been hugged*
*Eyes had seen human monsters,*
*destroying human beings*
*I cried, cried, cried*
*It wasn't roar but*
*Crying loud*
*Sometimes, tears must flow*
*until the face is dry,*
*Cry until tears run out.*

*Strength is found*
*in letting tears rain,*
*Let them shed with all sufferings,*
*Healing wounds with pain*

*comes boldness*
*Birth of confidence*

# *FAITH*

*No weapon stronger*
*to win against the bitter world,*
*But faith*

*No bullet strikes truer,*
*killing the enemy*
*without a grave decline,*
*But faith*

*Where faith arrives,*
*Self-doubt fades*
*Lamenting souls heal,*
*Faith don't belong to crying hearts,*
*But those that cried and laughed*

*Faith unlocks power's gates,*
*I've seen heroes,*
*icons, praised like gods,*
*are just humans*
*Had nothing bigger than faith,*
*Rising from ashes*

*Faith, a rose in deserts,*
*grows without water*
*Begins hope, builds esteem,*
*Confidence in a faithful heart,*

*Ends failure, begins success.*

# MY SOUL

*My soul,*
*You don't need race*
*All you need is*
*rest in peace while alive*
*Just breathe, stay alive*
*Fear not dark clouds,*
*nor the strong wind*
*Do not be a drifter*
*drifting in a sea of violence*
*Stand still and fight*

*My soul,*
*Stay alive, live again*
*Strength is your life*
*Rely on yourself*
*Even in death,*
*Leave a mark on the rock,*
*For great-grandchildren to see*
*your power*

*My soul,*
*Frightened souls seek refuge*
*but stand strong, face the fire*
*No matter the breaks,*
*Scars on your skin,*
*Defeats faced,*

*Stay unmoved*
*You are tough*

*My soul,*
*Indestructible*
*Powerful to power*
*Dangerous to danger*
*The world's most dangerous weapon*
*You can turn the world upside*
*You're untouched,*
*Burning like fire,*
*You're undefeated*
*when you aren't in the crowd*
*but alone*
*thinking and observing*

## *HUNGER*

*How painful the body feels,*
*How fast the brain works,*
*Though I'm tottering*
*I'll go through this tide*
*The most terrible enemy,*
*men thought they have sent me*
*Hunger*
*The truthful friend I ever had*
*Hunger*

*Like scorpion venom,*
*Hunger turns the body into*
*a restless, crazy thing*
*When the stomach is empty,*
*the brain leads me into action*
*Nothing awakens the spirit*
*like hunger*
*Those who know its power,*
*stand still in stormy winds*
*Unafraid of thunder*
*It's hunger*

*In what seems the world's end*
*An empty stomach strengthens my morale,*
*Standing strong like desert pyramids*
*Those who've tasted hunger*

*Survive any drought.*
*It's hunger*

*The conquering king,*
*Hunger that triggers anger,*
*that breaks rocks*
*A hungry man carves paths*
*through rocky mountains,*
*to reach green land*
*It's hunger*

# *NEVER STRIVE TO BE SEEN*

*I never sweat, never hustle,*
*Never strive to be seen by people*
*Can fight and reach the mountain peak,*
*I don't know who will care in the valleys,*
*When I'm on the top,*
*they might clap and smile,*
*But like seasons they change*
*I don't know who will remain good to me*
*when I will have been scarce*
*I don't know who really loves me*
*I know many who hate me*

*I never sweat, never hustle,*
*Never strive to be seen by people*
*They might be clapping*
*within they are rapping*
*They might congratulate though,*
*within they criticize*
*Like chameleons,*
*they resemble what they reach*
*Like a chameleon,*
*with eyes turning back,*
*I see their knives poised,*

*I never sweat, never hustle,*
*Never strive to impress people*

*I never strive be seen by a man*
*who strives to talk*
*I'm judging actions, not words,*
*Never striving to be seen by those*
*far from nature,*
*Too small to tread on the ground*
*like insects*

*I never sweat, never hustle*
*I never aim to please any living man*
*Not the public, assemblies, systems,*
*Religions, or cultures,*
*Striving only to be seen by my heart,*
*My only leader*
*to let my brain's gaze fall on me,*
*My only friend*
*I strive to impress my children,*
*Ones who will be my third led*
*when I'm too old to walk*

## THE TRUTH

*Nothing sets a man free*
*like opening his mouth*
*and spit the truth out of it*
*He makes sovereigns*
*feel naked just like*
*Adam and Eve in the Eden garden*

*Truth softens rock*
*to be soft like a cloth*
*Truth is the truth,*
*A weapon that kills enemies,*
*when tanks failed*
*when a bullet can't*
*Truth freezes fire like an ice,*
*Finds a way like water*

*The only lie I'll tell*
*is the truth*
*I may stand alone*
*but stronger than gods*
*A troublemaker to liars,*
*Breaking those who suppress it*
*into pieces like shattered glass*

*I tell the truth, I am strong,*
*As long as I tell the truth*

# IN THE DAWN

*Still dark in the dawn,*
*Everyone asleep,*
*Dreaming*
*some sweet dreams*
*some darkest seasons,*
*I'm awake, working on my dreams*

*I dream in the day,*
*Work on my dreams in the night*
*Never stop dreaming in daylight,*
*Never stop stepping forward*

*No moment as great*
*as walking towards destiny,*
*For me, that's the dawn*
*when silence rules*

*All are sleepy,*
*half dead, half alive*
*while I'm living*
*Their silence motivates,*
*as they sleep, I act,*
*Feeling brain working fast like*
*a toddler's*

*I wake before dawn or sleep after,*
*Love seeing dew on my window*
*Surrounded by quiet*
*With a pen in hand,*
*spitting ink on my pad*
*Ideas born in the dawn*

# AS HE GROWS OLDER

*As he grows older,*
*All things tasteless*
*No interest in respect*
*No need for praise*
*Don't thank him for his good deeds*

*As he grows older*
*He's just truthful*
*His lips know no lie*

*As he grows older,*
*He's getting weak and weaker*
*He might need somebody beside him*
*That would be ones who*
*inside their veins run his blood*
*or he would be anyone whose*
*heart is filled with love*

*As he grows older*
*No future interest,*
*Sometimes the past catches him,*
*He can't live it anymore*
*God can't change it too*
*Today alone matters*
*Sunshine on him*

*As he grows older,*
*No fear of death*
*He can see it coming*
*He ain't know when or how*
*Only Death knows*
*He lets him come*

*As he grows older*
*and he's in health,*
*Peace more than in death*

*As he grows older*
*He ain't cry for favors*
*If he sowed,*
*He can reap now*

# MY MEDICINE

*I'm ill, very ill,*
*I can feel it*
*Life slipping*
*I'm dying*
*Breath's struggle,*
*panting for air*
*A fight to fight*

*No movement left to make,*
*Death's coming close*
*Laughing loud,*
*Echoes of his laugh,*
*ringing,*
*Noises in my ears*

*Death stands proud,*
*Nearing another claim,*
*He's clapping for himself*
*Nearly seizing me,*
*His prize,*
*An honest man*
*Bigger than trials*
*feared not life's trials*
*Conquered battles with love*

*Death smiles,*
*Stealing another*
*talented man from this world*
*Mad for justice,*
*Threat to a downpresser*
*A happy man*
*when people happy*
*Godly man healed souls,*
*Stabbed by the so-called*
*men of God*

*Life's clock ticking fast,*
*Running low, it feels,*
*Dying,*
*Medicine on my bedside*
*pill of life, hope revived,*
*My hand, get it, get it*
*I can have my medicine now*
*Pen and pad beside,*
*Writing another poem to heal*
*Free hearts*
*in words, in prose,*
*I can write*
*I write on,*
*Death lost me*

# SILENCE AND ALONENESS

The beginning of burning like fire,
Cold like ice in a freezer
I haven't been warm
until I was
alone and frozen,
Unable to move,
now I run,
warming the planet earth

Growing colder,
ever colder
In my icy room,
I was just the lonely thing
Can't be touched though,
needing warmth
Realizing,
No need for anyone's charm.
Not one to get close to me
They'd ruin my aloneness,
guiding me to loneliness

Wisdom gained in solitude's space,
melting that cold ice
with inner grace
I lit the fire out of me
I sweat and burn,

*In days of silence, lessons learned.*

*In silence and aloneness,*
*I have known what to speak,*
*who to trust*
*In silence and aloneness,*
*Page was read*
*after a page,*
*anger fled*
*In silence and aloneness*
*Unbreakable, unshakable, I stand,*
*From cold to fire,*
*My heart's command*

# *I KNEW THE END*

*From the start*
*I knew the end*
*Stood on ground*
*Head held high,*
*Towards*
*that mountain end*
*I aimed,*
*Knowing only*
*to survive the climb*

*From the start*
*I knew the end*
*Painful climb*
*I was tired,*
*Almost surrendering,*
*Yet driven, I knew,*
*I'd reach the summit alive,*
*Through blood and sweat*

*From the start*
*I knew the end*
*Exhausting struggle*
*Rocks threatening*
*Shaky steps*
*Fear of breaking,*
*But, for I knew the end,*

*Pushing on through*
*the storm's drenching.*

*From the start*
*I knew the end*
*It was heavily raining*
*In dense, mounting forests,*
*Wolves' hungry chase,*
*Fighting tirelessly because*
*I knew the end, come what may,*
*Why I climbed, I knew, day by day.*

*At last,*
*On top of that lofty height,*
*Knowing the end from the very start*
*In trials faced, in battles won,*
*I turned the end into a new start*

# MY WORLD

*I keep myself within myself,*
*In a world I created*
*My own world*
*Here,*
*I never drink their poison*
*No harm to others*
*Won't get misdirected*
*I direct myself*
*No misunderstanding*
*No command, no order*

*I keep myself within myself,*
*In a world I created*
*My own world*
*Here,*
*Peaceful as a butterfly*
*upon a sunflower's bloom,*
*Love you can give me is*
*in letting I stay*
*in my world*
*Hate you can give me is*
*in pulling me*
*to your gloomy world*

*I keep myself within myself,*
*In a world I created*

*My own world*
*Outside worlds so wild,*
*Man makes man*
*kill another man,*
*for what money can buy,*
*Sometimes for nothing*
*Yet here, in my world*
*No hurt dealt,*
*None felt,*
*In my world,*
*Peace does reign*

*I keep myself within myself,*
*In a world I created*
*My own world*
*Away from your terrifying world,*
*Threatened me since birth*
*Escape found in death,*
*To rise again, in my world's stead*
*I'll dwell here, never to leave,*
*In my world, made by my heart*

# HOW I THINK

*I was taught of what to think*
*since I was a toddler*
*until I taught myself*
*how to think*
*I am always in love*
*with the way I think*
*Can't let me betray myself*
*No external impression*
*It's the only mindset*
*I lay within me*
*like a heart in the body*
*The way I think*
*makes me look within as*
*I look myself in a mirror*
*My real image's revealed,*
*I see the reality*
*I see the truth*
*I see the natural me*
*I never stand beside the tree*
*bears thorns, no fruits*
*I never lend my ears*
*to the beliefs with myths*
*That's a religion*
*I see them,*
*training human beings*
*how to think*
*The brain full of religious thoughts*

*rarely find knowledge*
*Sometimes wisdom is*
*an abandoned bastard*
*I'm a man of the nature*
*I'm a man of creativity*
*This is how I think,*
*How I shall think tomorrow*
*I never follow*
*anyone's opinion*
*No system and no politics*
*No tribe and no culture*
*No religion*
*I need not a mask to wear*
*I let me face the cold wind*
*I need not a helmet*
*No arrow can go through my head*
*Unyielding, and unbending iron*
*Covering tough thoughts*
*How I think is*
*how I shall think,*
*till I drop dead*
*Then, you can teach me*
*You can preach me*
*You can change me*

## TIME TO WALK AWAY

*Where intoxicating friends*
*offer nothing but*
*intoxication to your mind,*
*Leisure and idiotic entertainment,*
*Knowledge drowned in alcoholism*
*Time to walk away*

*Where teachings*
*and beliefs*
*offer you nothing,*
*Demand tenths of your earnings*
*Sweat from your brow*
*Bones breaking in work*
*Working like a slave,*
*Time to walk away*

*Where your business*
*brings only money,*
*Contributes nothing to humankind*
*Time to walk away*

*When your earnings*
*load in another's pocket,*
*Calling him boss,*
*No growth,*
*Where time spent bowing down*

*month after a month*
*year after a year*
*Fearing, praising those who*
*received your knowledge, wisdom,*
*Time, strength,*
*body, life, money,*
*Time to walk away*

*When ruled to worship a flag,*
*singing an anthem*
*for a nation that doesn't serve you,*
*Trashes your opinion,*
*No care for you and you're*
*voting and voting,*
*for the rich to get richer,*
*you remain poor,*
*giving your less*
*Time to walk away*

# I KNEW NOTHING AT ALL

*I thought*
*I knew everything until*
*I realized knowing everything*
*is knowing nothing at all*

*I thought*
*I had it all*
*until I found out*
*I had nothing*
*I knew nothing at all*

*So many hugged me,*
*Smiled at me*
*Kissed me*
*Cuddled, caressed me,*
*I got to know*
*I never even got a handshake*
*I knew nothing at all*

*I fought alone,*
*Reached the top,*
*But was still crawling*
*if I never pulled no one up*
*I knew nothing at all*

*I traveled overseas,*
*Sat first class*
*beside kings,*
*Sipped red wine,*
*Thought I lived*
*everyone's dream until*
*I missed myself*
*alone and happy unconditionally,*
*I knew nothing at all.*

*Years of false knowledge*
*from false intellects*
*stayed in my veins,*
*I was turned into an idiot*
*I knew nothing at all.*

*I laughed at the man,*
*falling from the tree*
*Sat on my branch,*
*eating sweet fruits until*
*it cracked and I fell*
*I knew nothing at all.*

*I bought a car,*
*Drove the streets,*
*Thought something was wrong*
*with those walking,*
*then a fleeting accident*
*took my legs,*

*Now I sit in a wheelchair,*
*They still walk*
*I knew nothing at all*

## TORTUROUS PATH BUT LEADING TO PARADISE

*No doubt*
*I love walking alone*
*away from the crowd*
*Though it feels like a tough journey,*
*It's a blessing*
*Though my head feels pain,*
*It's a painkiller*
*A torturous world,*
*death swinging in my brain*
*A suicide mission to be alone*
*A torturous path but leading to paradise*

*No tears shed for me*
*No soul rejoices for me*
*Yet I'm suffering from inside*
*I'm to cast the suffering away*
*I chose to run away*
*from where I was placed*
*The noise of this silence screams loud*
*A suicide mission to be alone*
*A torturous path but leading to paradise.*

*Hell and heaven are against me,*
*world's hatred since birth,*
*Hunted side to side,*

*forced me to be their servant*
*I reject their masters,*
*I want this pain over social death*
*I must walk alone*
*Like a kamikaze,*
*A torturous path but leading to paradise*

## MARRIAGE

*Marriage,*
*The most boring school*
*a man ever attended*
*A mythical place*
*where a man learns to be a fool*
*while a woman plays the genius*

*Marriage is like*
*viper's venom in the blood,*
*he still loves the feeling*
*Marrying a woman*
*married to money*
*He is her wallet*
*She's his lust's cure*
*He calls it lovesick,*
*She calls him foolish*

*Marriage,*
*A man's mind shrinks*
*She yearns for emotions,*
*impressions, surprises,*
*He loses himself in sentiment*
*against men's fight*
*for changing the world*
*He's forgetting dreams*
*No longer creating*

*Marriage,*
*She is his challenger*
*Wants him to slave,*
*covering positive with negative*
*Forget his childhood dreams*
*End his legacy*

*Marriage,*
*One's world ends as*
*the other only receives*
*gains from one's sweat*
*while the other sits and talks.*

*Marriage dies*
*if friendship breaks*
*If he isn't her friend,*
*she isn't his either.*
*He isn't her love*
*She isn't his love*

*Marriage,*
*A sharp razorblade on his skin,*
*when she's anxious*
*at every change,*
*Trembling with troubles,*
*She mustn't burden him*
*when things fall apart*

*Marriage,*
*Dangerous for a man,*
*when she shows*
*She knows better*
*and he quarrels*
*She wants action,*
*not words.*

*In marriage,*
*People swallowed by whales*
*Now scream for help*
*Cannot be saved*
*Single, always peaceful*

# *THEM*

*They said,*
*I'm low*
*Yes, I played low*
*They said,*
*I don't get involved*
*I'm silent,*
*Perhaps, I'm dumb*
*Yes, I observed*
*They said,*
*I'm a timid ghetto boy*
*Yes, I was cold*
*They laughed*
*I stayed calm*
*They said*
*I'm useless*
*I knew they weren't useful*

*Now, I'm back*
*to my normality*
*beyond their madness*
*It's me they wanted*
*Now they complain that*
*I jump like a fish*
*fighting for breath on the shore*
*They don't realize,*
*they were fishing me to death*

*My cruelty is here now,*
*the beast in the forest*
*Now they say,*
*I ain't right*
*I don't talk right*
*I don't do right*
*They made me wrong*

*Until*
*the cost of living drops,*
*I won't turn back*
*Until*
*inequality is a memory,*
*I'll do them wrong*
*Until*
*they stop feeding us hunger*
*while we pay them to eat,*
*I won't do right*
*I'll storm the gates,*
*I'll tide the land.*
*Until*
*all homeless have roofs,*
*pillows below their heads,*
*I'll still do wrong*
*Until*
*none of us are hungry*
*because they stored food,*
*I'll remind them they're not right*
*till we in ghettos can sleep*

*I hear them say*
*I'm a rebel*
*I say, yes,*
*Because I'm labored*
*They say,*
*I'm not above the law*
*I say, I'm lawless.*
*They threaten with jail*
*I say yes,*
*I've never been free*
*even if walking the streets*
*They said,*
*I'll die*
*I say yes,*
*Our women aren't barred.*

*Stand with me now,*
*We both face the situation*
*We need recognition*
*We need life right because*
*we're the living*

# A TAXMAN

*I never knew my father*
*Never heard a man call me "son"*
*He was gone before I was born*
*and at eleven,*
*I lost my mother too*
*A boy like me, out on the streets,*
*where a taxman was cruising*

*Hunger, my enemy*
*I ate from trash on Christmas day,*
*Drank unclean water,*
*The taxman was indulging*
*in Beluga fish and*
*sipped on wine*

*I got sick with no treatment*
*I didn't die,*
*The taxman was insured*

*School was never a dream,*
*A place for those with silver spoons*
*The taxman's daughter,*
*looked beautiful in her uniform*

*I slept in parks, on cardboard,*
*Cold but snoring*

*While for the taxman,*
*another comma was added*

*In rain, I hid under bridges,*
*awake till morning*
*I saw the luxury cars,*
*Taxmen heading to collect more*

*I cleaned restaurants for food*
*Carried loads for pennies*
*Tired like an old man*
*The taxman was around in the city*

*At fifteen, I realized*
*no one would remember me,*
*Not even if I died*
*I had to save myself*
*I worked for wages,*
*Fast and courageous*
*like a horse in a war*
*The taxman fitting in suits and ties*

*At twenty,*
*I rented a room,*
*Knew it for five hours a day*
*The taxman smelled the sea*
*every weekend,*
*Belly up in the sun,*
*cold drink on one side,*

*a beauty on the other*

*At twenty-five,*
*I started a business from my struggle*
*The taxman was the first to step in*
*"You must pay taxes or we close your shop."*
*I paid*

*Still spirited,*
*Still a hustler*
*I worked like hell,*
*Speeding with time,*
*like an impala running for water*
*I bought a house*
*A street child owning a home*
*The taxman knocked,*
*"You must pay the property tax."*
*"For what?" I asked*
*"The land belongs to the government," he*
*said,*
*Confident,*
*as if a man born holding soil*

*Now, I do as you do,*
*paying more for the taxman,*
*who vacations abroad,*
*builds mansions,*
*buys lands and businesses*
*He has money*

*Seems,*
*he can sail his heart to paradise,*
*leaving me in hell*
*I didn't realize,*
*all my childhood's sufferings*
*were in the interest of a man*
*who closed his eyes*
*when a homeless kid like me*
*begged for food*

# *HUNGRY*

*I'm hungry*
*Brother's hungry*
*Neighbors are hungry*
*Our children are hungry*
*Cost of living's beyond our wages*
*Taxes rising*
*Bread for the baby*
*A man stays hungry*
*Tomorrow's workday*
*I'll think badly*
*Grind deathly*
*Get angry*
*Act wildly*
*Thinking of the baby's life*
*I can shatter the world*
*Break through walls*
*of this darkest tunnel*
*to see another day*
*Children need food*
*Men keep men hungry,*
*driving them mad*
*I swear on earth's life,*
*I won't fade,*
*walking in a man's shade*
*seeing us as roaches*
*Men in offices,*

*I feel it in their breath*
*See it in their eyes*
*Sense it in their walk*
*They want me hungrier,*
*Work like a machine*
*till the last breath*
*My child doing the same*
*till the last breath*
*Yesterday I saw*
*my dearest neighbor,*
*Hunger gave him the worst death*
*I guess I'm next*
*They stock more than needed,*
*Trash cans fed*
*They go on vacation*
*after a day of taxation*
*It is exploitation*
*I'm still hungry*
*Now I'm angry*
*War against the wealthy*
*for my family*

# *IN THE END*

*In offices,*
*They fit in uniforms of honor,*
*their boys fit in uniforms of terror,*
*terrorizing for fun,*
*for oil, for gold*
*but in the end,*
*We are all the meal for earthworms*

*Our peace is their trouble,*
*they need more victims,*
*they're happy when we grieve*
*maybe the land thirsts for blood,*
*but in the end,*
*We are all the meal for earthworms*

*They were hunting in the past,*
*They're hunting today,*
*We are the prey*
*Killing is their work,*
*maybe their work for living*
*One who kills shall die too,*
*In the end,*
*We are all the meal for earthworms*

*No child was breastfed*
*the skills of pulling a trigger,*

No mother fed a baby
the science of atomic energy
Since man invented fire,
He's yearned to burn
We're burned,
but in the end,
We are all the meal for earthworms

In the morning,
a child used to bless eyes on the sun
In the evening,
used to smile with the sinking moon
Now the sun mourns,
The moon cries,
He's an orphan
Men in choppers return
Wives and children are waiting
Their country has won
Waving flags
but in the end,
We are all the meal for earthworms

A lion eats a zebra,
No more hunger
No more killing today
A hyena finished a kangaroo,
No more hunger,
No more killing today
Man owns the forest,

*The whole world in his pocket*
*The whole food in his stomach,*
*He's still hungry*
*He kills another man*
*but in the end,*
*We are all the meal for earthworms.*

*A man gives an order*
*Bombs rain on us*
*A neighbor's baby is gone,*
*He forgot he was ever a baby*
*Forgot, in the end,*
*We are all the meal for earthworms.*

## DEAD DREAMS

*Heading home from work*
*Three of us are workers*
*Struggling to survive*
*We're surviving*
*for our babies' sake*
*We once had big dreams*
*Childhood luxuries*
*Pots of gold*
*In the hood,*
*stars shone on our lineless faces*
*I would be a movie star,*
*He'd be a famous athlete,*
*and the other, a wealthy businessman*
*Now we are tired,*
*Heavy like punching bags*
*Pain in our shoulders*
*Lumbago in our backs*
*We're stepping stones*
*to someone else's dreams*
*Ours have turned into nonexistent,*
*and I'm getting old,*
*It's clear in my face*
*For twenty years,*
*I've fought to put food on the table,*
*still fighting*
*I look at my child's face,*

*He looks at me,*
*reading what's coming for him*
*I won't let it happen,*
*But how?*
*He has the right to live,*
*and living isn't being used*
*When a tool is old and rusty,*
*it's replaced*
*Our sons shouldn't be used*
*Time to save their future is now*
*Their dreams shall come true*
*Let no one make your child*
*an instrument like they did to us*
*Let no dreams die*
*like ours did*
*Give a child the best*
*He will only have it*
*when we've done our best*
*and beyond the best*
*Let's do it.*

## *WHAT GOD*

*I thank God,*
*I thank God I wasn't born in Iraq*
*Father bombed*
*Mother fleeing with me*
*Perhaps I'd be dead,*
*Hunger killing me in the camp*
*A soldier or terrorist*
*shooting all my friends*
*What God would a childlike that thank?*

*I thank God,*
*I thank God I wasn't born in Congo*
*Running under bullets in the air*
*Losing parents in forests*
*Mother raped*
*Parents dead on their birth land,*
*where lives are less valued*
*than cobalt, copper,*
*Diamond, uranium*
*Children's lives gone*
*So you can own a computer,*
*Wear a necklace,*
*Use a phone.*
*A billionaire remains a billionaire*
*What God can such a child thank?*

*I thank God,*
*I thank God I wasn't born in Gaza*
*Soldiers from the so-called holy country*
*bombing babies,*
*injuring children*
*Filthy bloodthirsty goons see it happening*
*Blood and sweat is what they brought*
*to human beings*
*I wonder who that God is*
*such a child would thank*

*I thank God,*
*I thank God; I wasn't born a Native*
*American*
*My mother being sexually assaulted*
*She'd had died running for life*
*Father would had been shot*
*by Non-Native perpetrators,*
*Cleansing the whole ethnic for a land*
*that no man created*
*What God would that child thank?*

*I thank God,*
*I thank God I wasn't born in Rwanda*
*I'd have seen my mother butchered*
*A neighbor hunting me to death*
*No river but bloodstream*
*Mother, father, brother, and sister,*
*all gone*

*What God would that child thank?*

*I thank God,*
*I thank God I wasn't born in South Sudan*
*Ethnicity replacing humanity*
*Zealous youth gathering to kill youth,*
*Guns supplied,*
*brother killing brother*
*Mother and sister fleeing, drifting*
*I'd have died fighting for a politician too*
*I wonder,*
*What God would such a child thank*

# THEY WANT MORE BABIES TO FEED

*I'm hungry,*
*They're hungry too*

*Here,*
*Love's food aroma,*
*makes me hungrier*
*There,*
*Hatred's food cooked,*
*They want more babies to feed*

*Here,*
*I wash my hands with healing water,*
*to heal souls*
*There,*
*They wash hands in blood,*
*their usual way*
*They want more babies to feed*

*Here,*
*A bite on sympathy tastes sweet*
*There,*
*They swallow bitter intemperance,*
*mixed with spices of indifference,*
*and rage*
*They want more babies to feed*

*Here,*
*In soup of compassion,*
*morality's salt added*
*There,*
*Soup of cruelty,*
*their salt is wickedness*
*They want more babies to feed*

*Here,*
*I bite bread of peace,*
*I feel hearty within*
*There,*
*Violence's bread they bite,*
*They feel evil within,*
*They love devil*
*They want more babies to feed*

*Here,*
*I add unity's sugar in*
*a brotherhood's tea*
*There,*
*Division's sugar in enmity's tea*
*They want more babies to feed*

*Here,*
*I'm full,*
*Won't leave this table of safety*
*There,*

*They're full,*
*Won't leave their table of war*
*They want more babies at the table.*